SUPER-AWESOME SCIENCE

THE SCIENCE OF SPORTS

by Wendy Hinote Lanier

Content Consultant
Mark Walsh
Associate Professor, Exercise Science
Miami University

Core Library

An Imprint of Abdo Publishing
abdopublishing.com

abdopublishing.com

Published by Abdo Publishing, a division of ABDO, PO Box 398166, Minneapolis, Minnesota 55439. Copyright © 2017 by Abdo Consulting Group, Inc. International copyrights reserved in all countries. No part of this book may be reproduced in any form without written permission from the publisher. Core Library™ is a trademark and logo of Abdo Publishing.

Printed in the United States of America, North Mankato, Minnesota
042016
092016

THIS BOOK CONTAINS RECYCLED MATERIALS

Cover Photo: Aaron M. Sprecher/AP Images
Interior Photos: Aaron M. Sprecher/AP Images, 1; Julie Jacobson/AP Images, 4; Vincent Thian/AP Images, 7, 45; Mark Duncan/AP Images, 8; Science Photo Library/Newscom, 10; James Crisp/AP Images, 12; Daisuke Nakashima/AFLO/Icon Sportswire, 14; Shutterstock Images, 17, 31; Sean Simmers/PennLive.com/AP Images, 19; Joshua Sarner/Icon SMI CIF/Joshua Sarner/Icon SMI/Newscom, 20; Joshua Weisberg/Icon Sportswire, 22, 43; Greg Trott/AP Images, 24; David J. Phillip/AP Images, 26; Oliver Multhaup/AP Images, 29; Jan Woitas/Picture-Alliance/DPA/AP Images, 34; A. Ricardo/Shutterstock Images, 36; Keith Bishop/iStockphoto, 39

Editor: Jon Westmark
Series Designer: Jake Nordby

Publisher's Cataloging in Publication Data
Names: Lanier, Wendy Hinote, author.
Title: The science of sports / by Wendy Hinote Lanier.
Description: Minneapolis, MN : Abdo Publishing, [2017] | Series: Super-awesome science | Includes bibliographical references and index.
Identifiers: LCCN 2015960517 | ISBN 9781680782509 (lib. bdg.) |
    ISBN 9781680776614 (ebook)
Subjects: LCSH: Sports--Juvenile literature.
Classification: DDC 796--dc23
LC record available at http://lccn.loc.gov/2015960517

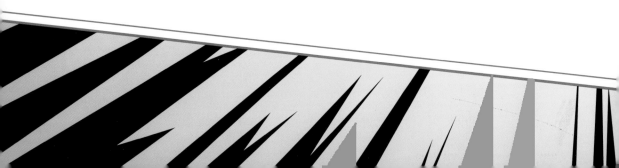

CONTENTS

CHAPTER ONE

MORE THAN MEETS THE EYE

It's the World Series—the bottom of the ninth inning. The team at bat is down by one run, and there are two outs. The count is one ball and two strikes. The pitcher winds up and delivers a pitch. As he releases the ball, he flicks his wrist to spin it. During the ball's flight toward the plate, the laces disturb the air. This creates high pressure on top of the ball and low pressure below it. The ball starts to drop. Then

Pitchers use the laws of aerodynamics to throw pitches that are difficult for batters to hit.

IN THE REAL WORLD

The Physicist Who Studied Tennis

Howard Brody was a University of Pennsylvania physicist who loved tennis. When oversized rackets were introduced in the 1970s, Brody tested them. He found the percussion center, or sweet spot, was closer to the center on larger rackets. This made them easier for players to use. Brody also proved it was better for rackets to be stiffer and for their strings to be looser than previously thought. This created a greater transfer of energy between the racket and the ball. The strings stretch more on impact. This allows more of the energy to return to the ball.

it drops even more. The batter takes a swing and misses. Strike three! The game is over. Science has helped the pitcher throw the perfect pitch.

All sports, including baseball, depend on the laws of science. Athletes are experts at using the laws of science to their advantage, even if they do not know they are. The sports we love involve more than aerodynamics, or how things move through the air. They involve many other

Science can help athletes establish good habits that help them during competition.

aspects of physics, as well as biology, chemistry, and psychology.

Chemical Makeup

It may seem obvious that biology plays a big role in sports. After all, biology is the study of living things, and athletes are living things. That makes their training, medical treatment, and nutrition all part of the game. People who study the biology of sports

Scientists and engineers work to protect football players from head injuries by creating better helmets.

are part of a field called sports medicine. They play an important role in keeping athletes healthy and performing at their best.

Chemistry also plays a role in sports. Chemistry is the study of what substances are made of. Sports scientists use chemistry to make and improve equipment. They also use chemistry to help decide what foods athletes should eat. Chemistry can help athletes perform at their highest levels. It can also help keep athletes safe.

The Physics of the Matter

Physics is the study of matter—how it moves, and how it responds to forces. Physics can explain the hang time of a quarterback's pass. It explains why long jumpers pump their arms like windmills during a jump. And it can even answer the question of whether to use a wooden or aluminum bat. Physics explains why sports work the way they do.

Biomechanics is one part of physics. It is the study of the way living things move and react to forces

Sports and Food

Sports nutritionists are part of a team that works with athletes to help them perform their best. Nutritionists study metabolism and nutrients for sports performance, and they study how to prevent disease. Metabolism has to do with how the body burns energy and manages the tissues that support life. The foods we eat provide the energy needed to support breathing, heart rate, and basic life activities. Sports nutritionists learn about what calories and nutrients athletes need to perform certain activities.

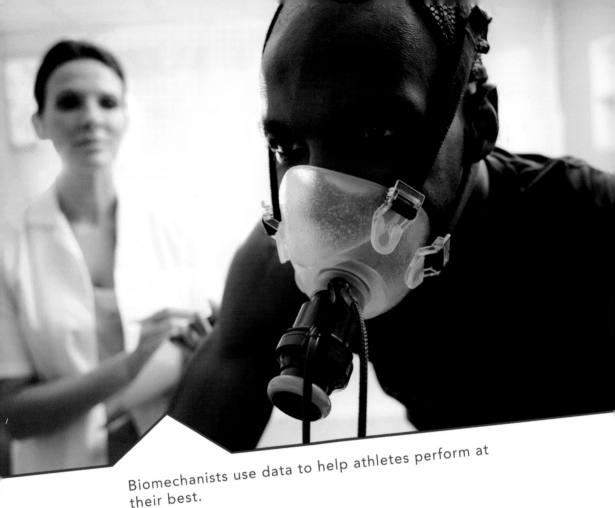

Biomechanists use data to help athletes perform at their best.

inside and outside the body. Biomechanists study muscles, bones, and joints to see how they respond to certain conditions. They help find the most effective movements to produce the best results.

In some sports, professional athletes have whole teams of biomechanists working with them to perfect their movements. Sticking a landing or making it over the high bar depends on making the right moves at the right times. Small adjustments in those movements can be the difference between winning and losing.

Healthy Mind, Healthy Body

Psychology is the study of the mind and how people think and behave. Sports psychology focuses on the minds and behaviors of athletes. Sports psychologists study the mental factors that affect athletic performance. They also study the ways participating in sports affect a person's mental and physical health.

Sports psychologists help athletes at all levels to perform better and handle the stress of competition. Sometimes they work with athletes who are having problems, but they also help athletes stay motivated. In addition, sports psychologists work with athletes recovering from injuries. These scientists help athletes enjoy their sports while maintaining good mental health.

Sports psychologists help athletes deal with the mental challenges they encounter in and out of competition.

Learning about science helps us better understand our world. In the case of sports, it unlocks the secrets of what makes the greatest athletes successful.

Many athletes today gather scientific feedback to improve performance. Shawn Heidgen is a coach and former women's cycling champion. In an interview, she talked about how modern technology affects training:

> With the help of some great coaches, we created a very specific and focused training plan. . . . Everything and anything I could measure I did and recorded it all. All hand written back then, but the knowledge I gained was priceless. I learned what I could handle, what was too much, and how to make every workout count. The data allowed me to come up with measurable and attainable goals. Eventually, I was able to compete on a national and even international level despite only being able to do a fraction of the training that most of my competitors were doing. . . . [W]hen you start tracking and analyzing your data, it is like getting glasses for the first time. Suddenly, everything is clear and in focus.

Source: Carrie Cheadle. "The Science of Sport—Interview with Shawn Heidgen of TrainingPeaks." Carriecheadle.com. Carrie Cheadle, March 26, 2015. Web. Accessed January 30, 2016

What's the Big Idea?

What is the main idea of this selection? Write down the main idea and list two or three details the author uses to support it.

CHAPTER TWO

BALL SPORTS

Many of today's popular sports are played with balls. The balls come in different sizes and materials. In ball sports, energy is transferred from a bat, arm, foot, club, or racket to a ball. The energy is transferred when a player hits, throws, or kicks the ball. The amount of energy depends on how much force is applied to the ball and how the ball is constructed.

Soccer players must be able to strike soccer balls with both accuracy and force.

Baseball: America's Pastime

A baseball pitcher's goal is to throw a ball that the batter cannot hit into the strike zone. Pitchers grip and release pitches differently to change how the ball flies. The goal is to catch batters off guard so they are not able to hit the ball.

One of the most important pitches in baseball is the fastball. Fastballs have backspin. Backspin makes the air flow more easily over the top of the ball. This is because the air moves in the same direction as the spin of the ball. When the air reaches the backside of the ball, it wraps around the ball before continuing on.

On the bottom side of the ball, the air flows in the opposite direction of the spin of the ball. This spin keeps the air from wrapping as far around the backside of the ball. Because more air on the backside of the ball travels downward than upward, the air behind the ball gets a downward force. Accordingly the ball receives the opposite force. If gravity weren't

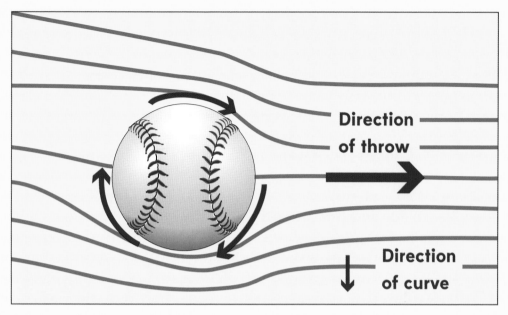

Spin and Curve
A curveball uses topspin to curve downward. How does the airflow behind the ball change? From what you've read in the chapter, how does this make the ball curve?

pushing it down, the ball would rise. Even with gravity pushing down, fastballs tend not to drop as far as other pitches.

Curveballs have topspin. Topspin creates an upward force in the air behind the ball. An opposite force acts on the ball. As a result, curveballs drop even more than they would with only gravity acting on them. Baseball pitches always curve in the direction the ball is spinning. This is called the Magnus effect.

Sliders and screwballs have sidespin. They move sideways as they approach the plate.

Batter Up!

On the other end of a pitch is a batter waiting to swing. The batter's goal is to transfer the maximum amount of energy to the ball. To do this, the batter must hit the ball at a certain spot on the bat. This sweet spot produces the most energy transfer. If the ball connects at the wrong place, less energy is transferred to the ball. This creates vibration within the bat. A good hit results in the ball having the greatest amount of energy. It also produces very

Pitchers apply pressure with the tips of their fingers to create spin and curve on their pitches.

little vibration in the bat. A batter barely feels the ball hit the bat on a good hit because the bat does not vibrate. Fans watching the game can hear a difference too. A ball that hits the sweet spot has a sharper sound than one that does not.

Wooden bats can splinter if too much vibration is transferred to the bat at contact.

As the ball flies off the bat, forces of gravity and air resistance continue to work to bring it to the ground. Mathematically it is best to hit the ball at a 45-degree angle. This angle maximizes the horizontal distance the ball travels in the air. But in reality, wind resistance and spin also play a role. Many players hit the ball at a lower angle. The ball rises because of backspin, helping to maximize distance.

Football Physics

Footballs travel differently through the air than baseballs. The football's oblong shape makes it unstable in the air. To counter this, quarterbacks spin the ball when passing. Doing so helps the ball travel smoothly instead of tumbling end over end. The ball spins around an imaginary line running lengthwise through the center of the ball. Scientists call this the gyroscope effect. The effect makes the ball

Which Bat?

Wooden bats are usually made of white ash or maple. Most metal bats are made of aluminum. Balls hit with aluminum bats go approximately 10 percent farther under equal conditions. One reason players can hit balls farther with aluminum bats is because the bats are lighter. They can be swung at greater speeds. Aluminum bats also have thin walls and are hollow. Wooden bats are solid. When a ball hits a wooden bat, the ball compresses. This makes the ball lose energy. When a ball hits an aluminum bat, the wall of the bat compresses. It acts like a spring and returns much of the energy to the ball. Professionals use wooden bats for safety reasons.

Spinning the football allows quarterbacks to throw the ball with speed and precision.

more stable in flight and helps it go farther. The more wobble the ball has, the shorter it will travel. This is because when a football wobbles, it exposes more area to the wind. Air resistance slows it down.

The rules of physics also apply to punting. Punters usually kick footballs at angles greater than 45 degrees. Steeper angles give punts more hang time. The longer a punt stays in the air, the more time defenders have to run downfield and tackle the punt returner. Most punters do not kick spirals. Putting sidespin on the ball might make it go farther in the air, but putting end-over-end spin helps the ball bounce forward when it lands. End-over-end punts also tend to be more difficult to catch.

Tackling is all about physics too. It involves a player's center of mass. A person's body rotates easiest around his or her center of mass. In most people, the center of mass is around the waist when standing upright. If a defender hits a ball carrier near the player's center of mass, the player is less likely to rotate. The ball carrier's legs will stay underneath the center of mass, allowing the player to stay upright. But if the defender hits the ball carrier farther from the center of mass, the player will rotate more. This is why many players try to tackle opponents low. Doing so rotates the ball

Crouching lowers a blocker's center of mass, making the person more difficult to push over.

carrier's body more. It also takes the person's legs out from underneath the center of mass.

Blockers also use this principle. Instead of standing straight up to block, they crouch. This lowers the player's center of mass, making it harder for other players to rotate the defender off balance.

Following a playoff game in 2015, the New England Patriots were accused of using deflated footballs during the game. Deflated balls are easier to throw. The Patriots argued that the deflation was caused by temperature changes due to weather. The following article from *Business Insider* disagreed with their claim:

A 20-degree [11°C] temperature change could account for a one PSI [703 kg/m²] decrease in air pressure. But for the ball to decrease naturally by two PSI [1,406 kg/m²], it would have to undergo a temperature change of 40 degrees [22°C]. On the night of the game, the temperature never dipped below 48.9 degrees [9.4°C] before the balls were tested at halftime. For temperature to account for air pressure change, the balls would have had to have been inflated in a 90-degree [32°C] room.

Source: Tony Manfred. "The Theory that the Patriots Balls Deflated by Themselves is Full of Holes." Business Insider. Business Insider Inc., January 23, 2015. Web. Accessed January 31, 2016.

Consider Your Audience

Imagine your friend does not believe the Patriots deflated footballs during the game. Rewrite the passage so it is easier for your friend to understand. How does your writing differ from the original text and why?

SPEED SPORTS

In many sports, the most important element is speed. The main objective is to be the first one across the finish line. Sometimes the competition is a large field of opponents. And sometimes the athlete races individually and tries to beat a certain time. Running, cycling, and swimming are all examples of speed sports.

Swimmers work to perfect their strokes in order to travel quickly and efficiently through water.

Sprint to the Finish

Reaching top speed is especially important for sprinters. Sprints are short, so every stride that is not at top speed is costly. With each stride, sprinters apply force to the ground and the ground pushes back. To get up to speed most quickly, sprinters need to direct as much force as possible in the horizontal direction. Leaning forward helps. It puts the legs in the best position to direct the most force from each stride down the track. Of course, sprinters must apply

Sprinter Usain Bolt sets a new world record and wins a gold medal in the 100-meter dash during the 2008 Summer Olympic Games.

a force upward. Otherwise gravity will pull them to the ground.

Runners also must deal with rotational forces. Each step a runner takes causes the upper body to rotate. The body rotates away from the foot striking the ground. Runners swing their arms opposite their feet when they run. The two opposite motions help balance the rotational forces. This keeps runners going straight ahead.

Speed on Two Wheels

Fluid dynamics plays a huge part in the sport of speed cycling. Fluid dynamics is the way liquids and gases affect objects moving through them. Cyclists provide the force that makes their cycles move. As they move, air is constantly pushing back on them. This force is called drag.

To increase speed and slip through the air more efficiently, cyclists wear special helmets and clothing. The clothing is smooth and tight in order to decrease drag. Cyclists also use special

Depending on wind conditions, cyclists sometimes cover the spokes on their wheels to reduce wind resistance.

handles that force riders to bend low over their bikes. This allows air to pass around them more easily.

The bicycle is considered one of the most efficient machines ever made. But today's scientists are finding ways to improve its design for faster cycling. Some are designed with frames made of tear-shaped tubing, which helps air flow more easily over the bike. Tires are now much thinner. This means less of the bike's surface area touches the ground. Less contact with the ground reduces drag caused by the road.

Making a Splash

Competitive swimming is another speed sport that is all about reducing drag. Swimmers must cut through the water in the same way cyclists cut through the air. Water pushes back even more than air because it is denser than air.

A swimmer's goal is to get the most distance out of each stroke. In this way, the swimmer can maintain high speeds by using fewer strokes. To reduce drag, swimmers keep their heads low and let

The Style of Speed

Many athletes wear special clothing to increase their speed. Swimmers wear streamlined suits with a tight weave. These compression suits help increase blood flow to the athlete's muscles. They help align the swimmer's body to reduce drag. Tiny V-shaped ridges in the suit also help reduce drag. Swimmers even cover their hair to improve race times.

their hips ride high in the water. This makes the body more like a torpedo traveling through the water. With each stroke, the swimmer's hands enter the water with fingers pointed toward the bottom of the pool. Swimmers apply force to the dense water with their fingers, hands, and arms, propelling them forward. Swimmers also kick their legs to move themselves forward, but like the arm swing in running, leg kicks also help keep the body from rotating too far in one direction.

FURTHER EVIDENCE

Chapter Three discusses the science of speed in sports. What is the main point of this chapter? What are some of the details that support this idea? Visit the website below. What information is similar to what you learned in the chapter. What new information did you learn?

Science of Cycling
mycorelibrary.com/science-of-sports

CHAPTER FOUR

AERIAL SPORTS

Some athletes spend a lot of time in the air. They know how gravity and the laws of motion will affect them. They gracefully jump, launch, spin, and flip before finding a way to land on their feet.

Ollie Up!

Skateboarders are one kind of high-flying athlete. They take advantage of the laws of physics with every move. Skateboarders bend their knees as they skate.

Ski jumpers use principles of flight to help them soar through the air.

Mega-ramps allow skateboarders to gain extreme speed before flying off a quarter-pipe into the air.

This lowers the rider's center of mass and makes it easier to stay balanced. Their arms are usually extended to distribute body mass over a larger area. This allows them to shift their center of mass from side to side without losing balance.

When a skateboarder jumps into the air, it is called an ollie. An ollie begins when the rider jumps up. As the rider jumps, he or she puts extra force on the tail of the board. This makes the tail bounce off the ground and up to the rider's back

IN THE REAL WORLD

A High-Flying Sport

In 2014 Alan Eustace broke a world record by skydiving from more than 25 miles (40 km) above Earth. His trip to the ground took 15 minutes. During his free fall, Eustace reached a speed of 822 miles per hour (1,323 km/h). Eustace made the trip in a specially designed spacesuit with a built-in life support system. The suit had a special coating designed to protect Eustace from extreme temperatures and radiation. It was pressurized to support regular breathing and blood flow.

foot. The rider uses his or her front foot to guide the board until gravity brings them both down again.

Flip, Flop, Tumble

Gymnasts also spend a lot of time in the air. In tumbling routines, gymnasts perform gymnastic moves on a springy floor. These include high-flying spins and flips. Gymnasts start their routines by running forward. This creates kinetic, or moving, energy along a straight line. When gymnasts plant their feet on the floor to jump, much of their moving energy gets redirected upward. If they want to spin, they push off the ground at an angle. This creates torque. Torque is a force that causes rotation. As gymnasts go through the air, they spin along an axis. The closer their bodies are to the axis, the faster they can spin. If gymnasts spin upright, they can pull their arms into their sides to spin more quickly. Gymnasts can slow their rotations by extending their arms outward, allowing them to land.

The Physics of Pole Vaulting

In pole vaulting, the jumper first sprints forward, creating kinetic energy. As the jumper plants the pole in the ground and moves into the air, he or she slows down. But the jumper's energy gets stored in the bending pole. At the top of the jump, almost all energy from the pole is given back to the jumper. This is called potential energy. The jumper uses this energy when he or she falls to the mat. The energy then gets sent into the mat. Where in the diagram does the pole vaulter have the most potential energy?

Flying on Skis

Downhill skiers use the force of gravity to create the speed needed to zip down a mountain. Ski jumping, however, is more like flying than skiing. Ski jumpers spend much of their time in the air.

Ski jumpers begin at the top of a steep incline. Jumpers accelerate down the hill. They crouch to reduce drag from air resistance. Jumpers can reach speeds of more than 60 miles per hour (97 km/h) on the ramp.

At takeoff the jumpers straighten out their bodies, lean forward, and hold their skis in a V shape. The air rushing over the top of the body and skis has farther to go than the air flowing underneath. This makes the air above flow faster and creates lower pressure on the topside of the skier. Maximum lift

Disc Golf

Disc golf is played with different types of flying discs. When a player throws a disc, the air moving over the disc moves more quickly than the air below it. This creates low pressure above the disc, making lift. Differently shaped discs produce different amounts of lift. Putters are dome shaped, so the air going over the top of the disc must travel much farther than the air below it. This creates a big pressure difference, allowing the putter to float more. Drivers have a flatter shape with sharper edges. This produces less lift but allows faster flight.

is achieved by the combination of ski position and the angle of the skier's body.

In Awe

Athletes do not always think about the forces at work when they perform their amazing feats. They focus on the skills they need to master. But for sports fans, understanding how athletes masterfully use science to their advantage can help us appreciate their accomplishments. It can also help us understand the forces that act on us all every day.

EXPLORE ONLINE

The website below discusses most of the sports in this book. What information can you find that is discussed in the book? What new information did you learn about these sports? What are some of the other sports talked about on the website? What did you learn about them?

Exploratorium: Sports Science
mycorelibrary.com/science-of-sports

FAST FACTS

- Physics, biology, chemistry, and psychology all have major applications in sports.
- The Magnus effect allows athletes to throw, hit, or kick balls in a way that gives them curved flight.
- Baseball batters and tennis players try to strike the ball with the part of the bat or racket that transfers the most energy to the ball.
- Without spin and wind resistance, an object launched at 45 degrees will travel farthest.
- Football tacklers try to knock the ball carrier's legs out from underneath the player's center of mass.
- Sprinters, cyclists, and swimmers are always looking for ways to reduce drag.
- Sprinters pump their arms opposite their legs to balance their rotational forces.
- Swimmers position their bodies like torpedoes to increase their speed through the water.
- Kinetic energy is the energy of motion. Potential energy is stored energy.

- Gymnasts use torque in order to spin and flip through the air.
- Ski jumpers position their bodies so that high pressure develops underneath them, creating lift.

STOP AND THINK

Dig Deeper

After reading this book, what questions do you have about the science of sports? Is there a sport you enjoy that was not covered in the book? With an adult's help, find a few reliable resources that can help you answer questions about these or other sports. Write a paragraph about what you learned.

You Are There

Chapter Four discusses some of the science behind ski jumping. Imagine you are competing in the ski jumping event at the Winter Olympics. Write a letter to a friend describing how you feel before, during, and after your turn. Describe the sights and sounds as you prepare to jump, as you zip down the ramp, and as you sail through the air.

Why Do I Care?

You may be a sports fan, or maybe you play sports in school or in a league. How does what you learned about the science of sports affect your life? How will it change the way you view some sports? How might it change the way you play a sport?

Say What?

Reading about the science of sports can mean learning a lot of new vocabulary. Find five words in this book you've never heard before. Use a dictionary to find out what they mean. Then write the meanings in your own words. Use each word in a new sentence.

GLOSSARY

axis
an imaginary line that
something turns around

compress
to make shorter or smaller

force
energy used to cause
movement or change

gyroscope
a spinning object that
maintains its position in space
as it spins

horizontal
parallel to level ground

kinetic energy
the energy of motion

mass
the amount of matter a body
contains

metabolism
chemical reactions in cells
that convert food into energy

potential energy
the energy something has
because of its position, rather
than its motion

vibration
rapid motion back and forth

LEARN MORE

Books

Amazing Sports and Science. New York: TIME for Kids, 2014.

Mercer, Bobby. *The Leaping, Sliding, Sprinting, Riding Science Book: 50 Super Sports Science Activities.* New York: Lark, 2006.

Vizard, Frank. *Why a Curveball Curves: The Incredible Science of Sports.* New York: Hearst, 2008.

Websites

To learn more about Super-Awesome Science, visit **booklinks.abdopublishing.com**. These links are routinely monitored and updated to provide the most current information available.

Visit **mycorelibrary.com** for free additional tools for teachers and students.

INDEX

ABOUT THE AUTHOR

Wendy Hinote Lanier is the quintessential Texan and a former elementary teacher who writes and speaks for children and adults on a variety of topics. She is the author of more than a dozen books for children and young people as well as articles and devotions for children and adults in various publications.